DUDLEY SCHOOLS
LIBRARY SERVICE

KU-099-381

Schools Library and Information Services

S00000730764

How do eggs get to market?

Market

the
BIG
PICTURE

Catherine Chambers

730764   SCH
J915.4

Published 2010 by
A&C Black Publishers Ltd.
36 Soho Square, London, W1D 3QY

www.acblack.com

ISBN HB 978-1-4081-2792-6
       PB 978-1-4081-3159-6

Text copyright © 2010 Catherine Chambers

The right of Catherine Chambers to be identified as the author of this work has been asserted by her in accordance with the Copyrights, Designs and Patents Act 1988.

A CIP catalogue for this book is available from the British Library.

All rights reserved. No part of this publication may be reproduced in any form or by any means – graphic, electronic or mechanical, including photocopying, recording, taping or information storage and retrieval systems – without the prior permission in writing of the publishers.

Every effort has been made to trace copyright holders and to obtain their permission for use of copyright material. The author and publishers would be pleased to rectify any error or omission in future editions.

This book is produced using paper that is made from wood grown in managed, sustainable forests. It is natural, renewable and recyclable. The logging and manufacturing processes conform to the environmental regulations of the country of origin.

Produced for A&C Black by Calcium. www.calciumcreative.co.uk

Printed and bound in China by C&C Offset Printing Co.

All the internet addresses given in this book were correct at the time of going to press. The author and publishers regret any inconvenience caused if addresses have changed or sites have ceased to exist, but can accept no responsibility for any such changes.

Acknowledgements

The publishers would like to thank the following for their kind permission to reproduce their photographs:

Cover: Shutterstock: Jeremy Richards, David S Rose (front), Eric Isselée (back). **Pages:** Corbis: Caroline Penn 19; Shutterstock: Karoline Cullen 22-23, Dhoxax 10, 20, Tomo Jesenicnik 7, Girish Menon 2-3, 18-19, Galina Mikhalishina 10-11, Herr Petroff 20-21, Jeremy Richards 4-5, 8-9, 12, 12-13, 14-15, 16-17, 18-19, Dennis Albert Richardson 16, 24, Vishal Shah 4, 6-7, Smit 14-15, Becky Stares 3, 6, Tonis Valing 1, ZCW 8.

Contents

Market

Market **day in** India **is bright and busy. People buy and sell all kinds of things at the market.**

Meet Asha

"I live in a small village in India. My family keeps hens. I collect eggs from the hens and take them to the market."

Find out what happens to Asha's eggs.

For sale

Eggs, fruit, and vegetables are sold at the market. Shoes and clothes are sold there too.

Hi!

Asha's Hens

Some hens live in huge sheds. Others live in open fields, or the backyards of people's homes.

Asha says

"My family has nine hens. At night they live in a small hen house in our backyard."

Cluck, cluck!

Asha must feed her hens every day.

Hungry hens

Asha lets the hens out of their house before she goes to school. She gives them **seeds** to eat and water to drink.

Asha's Eggs

Asha and her friends collect the eggs on market day. How many will they find?

Asha says

"We have to hunt for the eggs – the backyard hens can lay their eggs anywhere!"

Asha puts the eggs in her basket.

Find the eggs!

Busy hens

A backyard hen in India lays about one egg each week. Hens in large sheds lay one egg a day.

Market Day

Carts and rickshaws **are often used to take things to the market.**

Asha says

"We put all our eggs into a large cart. My neighbours put fruit and vegetables in the cart too."

Rickshaws are piled high with things to sell at market.

NAYYAR GENERAL STORE

Off to market

Don't smash!

Big farms use trucks to take eggs to market. The eggs travel in boxes. The boxes have a safe pocket for each egg to stop them smashing.

Asha's Stall

Some market stalls are in big buildings. They stay there all the time. Other stalls are in streets or fields.

Asha says

"Our stall is on a street market. I help my mother to lay out all the eggs."

There are lots of eggs for sale at the market.

Busy, busy!

Look and buy

At street markets, people walk past each stall and choose what they want to buy. The stalls are taken down at the end of the day.

How Much?

Asha is selling hens' eggs, but some people sell ducks' eggs or huge ostrich eggs.

Asha says

*"We sell our eggs two at a time. Each egg costs 30 **rupees**. I put the eggs in small bags."*

Yum!

Lots of sweet things are also sold at the market.

All gone

Asha has sold all the eggs. Now she has some money to buy jalebis. These are bright orange sweets.

15

Look and See

You can see lots of fruit, vegetables, and flowers in a market.

Asha says

*"There are **radishes**, spinach, tomatoes, and lemons at our market. We use all of them in our cooking."*

Favourite flower

Huge baskets glow with bright yellow and orange marigold flowers. It is one of the most popular flowers in India.

Smells lovely!

You can buy lots of flowers at a market in India.

Spicy!

The market is bright with **red, yellow, green, and brown** spices. They make food very tasty.

Asha says

"My favourite spice is green cardamom. It is added to sauces, tea, and even ice cream."

We love spice

Some spices are sold as seeds. Others are ground into powder.

Get better

Spices can also help people when they are feeling ill. Yellow turmeric and brown cloves are used to make people feel better.

Time to Go

Market day is over. Everyone packs up their things. Then they pick up the rubbish.

Asha says

"We pick up used plastic bags. I wash them and they are used again the next market day."

Goods that are not sold are taken home again.

Making roads

Recycled plastic bags are used to make new, smooth roads in India. And that helps to stop eggs breaking on the way to market!

Home time

Glossary

India large area of land called a subcontinent. Many people live in India.

market place where lots of things are bought and sold. Markets can be inside buildings or outdoors.

ostrich large bird that does not fly

radishes small, red salad vegetables

recycled made into something else

rickshaws bikes that pull a cart at the back, in which people or goods can be carried

rupees coins used to buy things in India

seeds small parts of plants that can grow into new plants. Seeds can also be eaten for food.

spices ingredients that are added to food to make it taste good

Further Reading

Websites

This website will tell you more about India.
You can find it at:

kids.nationalgeographic.com/Places/Find/India

You can see more about India on this website.
Just click on the pictures at:

homefreeuk.net/elloughton13/india.htm

Find out more about chickens at:

www.kiddyhouse.com/Farm/Chicken/html

Books

India (Looking at Countries) by Jillian Powell,
Franklin Watts (2007).

India (Living In) by Rachel Thomson, Franklin Watts (2005).

Geeta's Day: From Dawn to Dusk in an Indian Village
by Prodeepta Das, Read Write Inc (2006).

Your Chickens: A Kid's Guide to Raising and Showing
by Gail Damerow, Storey Books (1993).

Index